To the nurses and docs of the Pennsylvania Hospital NICU—
you make the desert bloom
DE

Thanks to everyone working to protect the environment
and all of these amazing creatures
GW

ALSO BY DAVID ELLIOTT

On the Farm   *In the Sea*   *In the Wild*

On the Wing   *In the Past*   *At the Pond*

In the Woods   *At the Poles*

IN THE DESERT

DAVID ELLIOTT

ILLUSTRATED BY GORDY WRIGHT

CANDLEWICK PRESS

THE SAHARA

Sand and rock.
Nothing more
except the sun,
which blinds the sky
and scrapes the land
clean like a butcher
with his favorite knife.
Here there is white bone.

But here is also life.

THE DESERT HORNED VIPER

Why do
they call
this place
the Land
of Fear?

It is
because
they know
that you
are here.

THE FENNEC FOX

Above his sandy head
the desert stars
are glistening,
glistening.

Shhhhhhhh!
Shhhhhhhh!

The little fox
is listening,
listening.

THE SAHARAN CHEETAH

You are spotted.

As the sun sinks
in its dry, dark well,
the oryx, addax,
and gazelle question
the time on earth
they are allotted
and run—run,

you are spotted.

DEATHSTALKER SCORPION

You pack
a lethal punch
for such
a little fellow,
hiding there
beneath a rock,
two claws,
eight legs,
and yellow.

But you keep
a shocking secret
in your fierce
and stinging tail:

in defiance
of your name,
you stalk life as well.

THE OSTRICH

Long neck.
Strong legs.
Big bird.
Big eggs.

THE ANUBIS BABOON

You bark
and grunt.

You roar
and screech.

You yak
and click.

This is
your speech.

Not a breach
of etiquette,

but simply proof
that you have learned

the basic baboon
alphabet.

THE NILE CROCODILE

And what are you thinking of now, Old Grinner?

I'm thinking of you, my dear. I'm thinking of dinner.

DESERT ANTELOPES

The addax
is xeric
and also
the oryx.

It means that
they live
in the desert,
of couryx.

THE SAND CAT

She looks as if
she might just be
the family pet,
that is to say,
mild, domestic.
Yet like her
roaring cousins
to the south,
she is—
in her small way—
majestic.

THE DUNG BEETLE

How easy
to make
fun of
you. That
rolling
thing you
do? Most
would find
appalling.
How strange
your mean
and humble
calling. No
one would
guess your
lowly work's
determined
by the
stars. How
elegant!
How surprising!
How celestial
you are!

THE DESERT HEDGEHOG

Yikes!
Spikes!

THE PAINTED DOG

The artist that
created you
was surely in
a rush. She did
not use her brush
to paint

but

rather

to
splatter.

It doesn't matter.

Why should we care
when the result
is so astonishing,
so original,
so rare?

THE SAHARAN SILVER ANT

Every minute counts.
You have ten at best
to get to your food
and get back to your nest.

One more minute and
it could be your last.
The sands are burning.
Good thing you're fast.

THE NUBIAN VULTURE

Red of face
and black of wing
you descend

and we recall
that everything
must have its end:

every life,
every creature.
You are the desert's
hardest teacher.

NOTES ABOUT THE SAHARA DESERT AND THE ANIMALS

THE SAHARA: About the size of the United States and spreading across eleven countries in Africa, the Sahara is the largest hot desert in the world. When we think of the Sahara, most of us think of dunes. And no wonder! Dunes can be as tall as 500 feet (150 meters). But the dunes cover only about 15 percent of the Sahara. Mountains, plateaus, sand plains, and salt flats make up the rest.

THE DESERT HORNED VIPER: If you're walking in the Sahara, be careful where you step. This venomous sidewinder often buries itself in the sand so that only its eyes are visible. Those "horns" are actually single scales that protrude above each eye.

THE FENNEC FOX: These little creatures are the smallest of all the world's foxes. But what they lack in body size, they more than make up for with their ears, which can be up to 6 inches (15 centimeters) long. Those ears are not just for show, either. By radiating heat, they also help the foxes keep cool. Don't you wish your ears did that?

THE SAHARAN CHEETAH: Little is known about the rare Saharan cheetah, which is smaller than its cousins living in the savanna. Its coat is a pale creamy white rather than a vibrant orange, and its face often lacks the spots and tear stripes that other cheetahs are so famous for. This cheetah doesn't need to drink water. A carnivore, it can get all the moisture it needs from its prey.

DEATHSTALKER SCORPION: Formerly known as the yellow scorpion, the deathstalker lives up to its new name: its venom is one of the most dangerous in the world. But here's the thing: In that venom is a substance called chlorotoxin. Researchers are discovering that chlorotoxin is a powerful weapon against glioma, an aggressive type of brain tumor. Maybe in the future the scorpion's name will change again, from deathstalker to lifesaver.

THE OSTRICH: Weighing in at an average 330 pounds (150 kilograms), the ostrich is the world's biggest bird. That weight helps to explain why it can't fly. But don't worry. At a top speed of 45 miles (72 kilometers) per hour, an ostrich can outrun most of its predators. If one does happen to get too close, it had better look out. A kick from an ostrich can easily kill and disembowel a lion! Because of that strong kick, the ostrich is considered to be one of the world's most dangerous birds.

THE ANUBIS BABOON: When seen from a distance, this baboon's coat looks slightly green, which is why it is also known as the olive baboon. In addition to the many sounds mentioned in the poem, baboons also communicate nonverbally by flattening their ears, smacking their lips, sticking out their tongues, grinding their teeth, and even yawning. Why not try some of that at the dinner table tonight? If anyone objects, simply explain that you are speaking baboon.

THE NILE CROCODILE: The average length of the Nile crocodile is 16 feet (5 meters), but they have been known to max out at 20 feet (6 meters). (That's about the size of four average sixth graders lying head to foot.) Nile crocs are at the top of the food chain. In other words, they have no predators. Speaking of food, the diet of these giants consists mainly of fish, but they will eat just about anything that moves, including . . . er . . . people. Nile crocodiles are estimated to be the cause of nearly two hundred human deaths every year. Anyone for a swim?

DESERT ANTELOPES: It might be easy to confuse the addax and the scimitar oryx since both are desert-dwelling antelopes. But their horns tell the story: the addax has spiral horns, while the horns of the oryx are straight. Both can go for very long periods of time without drinking, getting most of their moisture from the plants they eat. Some people think that an oryx with a broken horn is a source of the myth of the unicorn.

THE SAND CAT: Very little is known about the elusive sand cat, in part because it's very hard for researchers to locate. Its footpads are covered with thick fur, ensuring that it leaves almost no tracks. Although the sand cat looks almost exactly like your neighborhood kitty, don't be fooled. This little feline, the only cat to spend all its life in the desert, is ferocious. Oh, and there's another difference, too, one that makes it more similar to a dog: it barks!

THE DUNG BEETLE: Dung beetles make their living by forming balls of the waste of other animals and rolling them back to their nest. Maybe that seems kind of gross. But think about this before you dis these tiny workers: they navigate the desert by the Milky Way, enabling them to find a straight line back home. Like GPS, but way cooler.

THE DESERT HEDGEHOG: Desert hedgehogs are the smallest of all the world's hedgehogs. But that doesn't mean they can't protect themselves. When they sense danger, they roll into a ball and flex their muscles. This causes their skin to tighten, which in turn causes the sharp quills on their back to stand up. If you're a predator, you can forget about it. Baby hedgehogs are called hoglets. A group of hedgehogs? An array.

THE PAINTED DOG: It might be easy to confuse a painted dog with a hyena, but they are completely different animals. For one thing, the hyena is more closely related to the cat family, while the painted dog's cousins are jackals, wolves, foxes, and domestic dogs. No two painted dogs have the same markings. They are one of the most endangered animals in Africa.

THE SAHARAN SILVER ANT: This ant's body is covered with tiny silver hairs that give it a gleaming metallic look. Because of the extreme heat in the Sahara, the ant can be out of its nest to look for food for only about ten minutes a day. But it makes good use of its time. It can run its own body length at about 108 times per second, making it one of the fastest insects on the planet. To understand how fast that is, imagine a human who could run 400 miles (640 kilometers) per hour.

THE NUBIAN VULTURE: The largest vulture in Africa, the Nubian is also known as the lappet-faced vulture because of the fleshy folds of thick pink skin, called lappets, that form on the back of its head. Vultures are carrion eaters. In other words, their main diet is the flesh of animals that have already died. Nubian vultures mate for life.